Cats in Love

Cats in Love

J.C. Suarès and Jane Martin

Welcome Enterprises, Inc.

New York

First Published in 1996 by Welcome Enterprises, Inc.
New York, NY

Distributed by Stewart, Tabori & Chang, Inc.,
a division of U.S. Media Holdings, Inc.
115 West 18th Street, New York, NY 10011

Distributed in Canada by General Publishing Company Ltd.
30 Lesmill Road, Don Mills, Ontario, Canada M3B 2T6

Distributed in Australia and New Zealand by Peribo Pty Ltd.
58 Beaumont Road, Mount Kuring-gai, NSW 2080, Australia

Distributed in all other territories by Grantham Book Services Ltd.
Isaac Newton Way, Alma Park Industrial Estate
Grantham, Lincolnshire, NG31 9SD, England

Library of Congress Card Catalog Number: 96-060753
ISBN 1-55670-507-7

Printed and bound in Italy by Arnoldo Mondadori Editore
10 9 8 7 6 5 4 3

Page 2:
THOMAS WESTER
Consolation at the Cat Show
Nybro, Sweden, 1984

Contents

I had a tuxedo cat named Lurch, a very dapper and aloof fellow who completely lost his cool when a certain gray cat moved into the neighborhood. She was young, petite, and shy, and had a habit of lying in our front yard, sweetly blinking in the bright southwestern sunlight, her tail waving slowly. At her arrival, Lurch, who would fight almost any cat for territory and hissed at humans as well, would collect himself, smooth down his fur, and put all his crotchety ideas behind. Then he'd slip through the screen door and quietly trot over. He'd come up to her carefully, sniff at her with a delicate gesture, and, when she didn't swat at him, lie down a few feet away, pointing entirely in her direction. All his attention was on her. If a fly caught her eye and she followed it with her sight, Lurch watched it too. If she rolled over and faced a different direction, so did he. If she got up to move to a shady spot, he got up and moved to a place the same distance away. This went on for days. I saw less and less of Lurch. When he was around, he picked at his food when he came in to eat, and pined by the front window, waiting for the gray cat to reappear. Finally he disappeared altogether. One night, I opened the front door to go sit on the porch, hoping I might see him. There he was, with his sweet gray cat, curled up together on the porch chair. She was fast asleep, but he woke to the noise of the door, raised his head, and shot me a look with a clear message. "Leave me alone," it said, "I'm in love." The general impression most of us have of cats is that, aside from man-made lore like "Puss in Boots," love is not really in their emotional vocabulary. Aloofness, maybe; independence, maybe; some superficial affection around mealtime, perhaps. But since their first days as domesticated animals in the Egypt of 2000 B.C. the presence of a cat has prompted reactions from worship to fear to loathing—rarely have cats been given the opportunity to just be themselves.

Considered on a more individual basis, the character of a cat changes completely. From this point of view, some cats are born sweethearts. Certain breeds and types, such as Maine Coons, Ragdolls, and Smokes, are known for their easygoing, affectionate demeanors; others, such as the Siamese, are known for their expressiveness. Medical studies with the old and infirm have proven that a cat can function as stress reducer and veritable lifesaver; in a recent study of Alzheimer's disease patients living at home with a cat, virtually all were found to have fewer episodes of aggression and anxiety (dogs, to their credit, had the same effect)—which enabled caregivers to do a better job. A California animal hospital, in an effort to help people with AIDS keep their longtime feline companions, offers free veterinary care. And in a recent psychological study of human-animal companionship, respondents cited cats' loving, affectionate natures as a primary reason to have one. Said one respondent to an on-line survey posted on the Internet, "When I come home, my cat is more excited to see me than the dog is." So much for the slinking prowler who hides from his owners by day and slips into a mystery world by night: cats, it seems, are saps. They can be attached, gregarious, needy, and even giving. As some of the experts surveyed in this book assert, feline love takes on myriad dimensions, including everything from compassion to obsession. "Cats may not think of sex and lust the way we do: for them, mating is a function," says animal behaviorist Marge Beebe, "but affection, bonding, dependency, and choosiness are all part of their behavior."

Perhaps we can't really acknowledge love if it doesn't seem to stem from the hapless romanticism that marks our version. But as anthropologist Elizabeth Marshall Thomas points out, "friendship-based love is the glue that holds all of us together—and cats too. One kind of love is more stormy, the other is more profound. Perhaps we could say that cats are more profound." It is sheer arrogance, Thomas says, to think that cats do not feel love. "We're mammals, cats are mammals." she adds. "We all have these feelings because we are mammals, not because we are people. And think of it: love has powerful evolutionary value." Perhaps that explains why so many cat owners have been struck by the sense that there was a clear channel between themselves and their cat. We are not as far apart, considering evolution's timeline, as we might think.

Whatever viewpoint one takes, the case for what cats feel has some indelible examples. Consider Polar Star—thrown rudely out of his house at the end of a vacation season—who saw fit to shower his affection on a whole slew of people when brought to Cleveland Amory's office at the Fund for Animals. Or Josephine, the philosopher's cat whose utter dependency on her owner triggered his recovery. Or the Grinch and the Burmese, two social outcasts who found each other in a veterinary clinic and have been together ever since.

There are famous examples as well. In Hollywood's roaring twenties, Mack Sennett's renowned comedy troupe featured a comedienne cat named Pepper—a gray alley cat who wandered onto the set one day and became an overnight fixture: she was so attached to her costar, a Great Dane, that when the big dog died she walked off the set in grief and never acted again. The Oakland, California, firestorms of 1991 produced amazing stories of the cats who came back. More recently, a true tale of an orange kitten and a grizzly bear in Oregon made both celebrities—with Hollywood watching, of course. Cats, one expert argues, come in so many different personalities even within a specific breed that they could easily strike up an enduring bond with another animal—and that can include humans as well. So the Oregon pair is not so different from the Manhattan Siamese who greets her returning owner with an operatic barrage, or the Kentucky barn cat that befriended a nervous horse, or the white kitten who treats bunny rabbits like siblings. And cat à cat, the affinities are just as varied: kitten-fickle, brief as a full moon, or enduring as a lifetime. Anything is possible.

Perhaps the mythic feline that inspired the Egyptians and inflamed the Salem witch-hunters is not so far from the truth: the lore attests to our trying to pin down a creature that's at once inscrutable and emotional, entirely familiar and eerily unsettling. But once you get to know them, cats reveal an even more common characteristic: heart. No one can prove that a cat has nine lives—particularly a grieving owner. But we could venture to say that endowing one creature with so many lives is our way of acknowledging their tremendous spirit. Faced with change or loss, cats endure. They never lose their capacity to love.

—JANE MARTIN

THOMAS WESTER
Untitled
Stockholm, Sweden, 1984

Beau

Thomas Wester
In Love
Smogen, Sweden, 1983

Until recently I had Sasha and Beau, her son. When I got Sasha she was a skinny little black cat and I had no idea she was pregnant. Actually, neither did the vet. Months later she had kittens. Beau, the gray-and-white one, stayed. He never had to leave his mother, though she wound up leaving him. Every time I came home I'd find them hugging each other on the bed, wadded together in a ball, completely a unit. Sometimes they'd spoon. When she lay down he'd walk over, lie next to her, and put his head on her lap. He was always the baby: when they were wrestling, if she got too rough on him he'd just give up and complain.

When she got sick, he freaked. That was the hardest part. He got really aggressive towards her— he'd growl when she walked towards him, as if he didn't recognize her. Maybe she smelled bad— of shots and medication. When she got too close, he'd hide under a chair. At the very end when she was really out of it, I'd bring her up on the bed for a while and when she was lying there next to me, he'd lie next to her like he used to. But I think it was because she wasn't threatening. She was still and quiet.

There were two periods of time when she was at the vet for a few days and came home again, and he was fine. But the first day she was really gone, he sat alone in the middle of the room and cried out for her like he used to as a kitten, waiting for her to call back to him. Then he seemed to realize he wasn't getting an answer, and stopped. He's eight years old now and I'm starting to see a change. He's even more demanding of attention, only now it's from me. When I'm getting ready to leave for work, he winds himself around my legs and tries to hold me up. I'm very understanding about it. We both miss his mother. I can still see her looking at me, waiting to steal my food. Beau, bless him, is entirely uninterested in food. He just wants love.

PATRICIA FABRICANT, ART DIRECTOR

The Love of a Pride

THOMAS WESTER
Fence Romance
Dalhem Gotland, Sweden, 1984

My Maine Coons always surprise me. They're pride cats, descended from wildcats in Maine. Most domestic cats are descended from North African wildcats, which were lone hunters. Maine's wildcats live in prides, and not only accept each other's company, they want it. To make a stronger distinction think of dogs, who are pack animals. A pack animal will find a morsel of food and steal away so he can eat it all by himself. A pride animal will bring it back for everyone else. My cats not only bring home the bacon, they make a big show of it and invite each other to share in the wealth. Then they lie in happy heaps and just purr.

I had a kitten who once got into a big mess and I had to wash him off. So I took him over to the sink and started rinsing his fur. I was very gentle but a kitten is a kitten and he started to scream. All the other cats heard him. Before I knew it I was surrounded by the pride. They were so concerned that they tried to stop me by putting their arms around my legs. If you've ever felt a cat put their arms around your leg, you know the message. It's "Stop, right now. I insist." I had a choice: risk scratches and worse, or stop. I got the kitten rinsed off enough to be safe, and put him down. Immediately, the pride ushered him into the next room and began to clean him themselves.

MARGE BEEBE, ANIMAL BEHAVIORIST AND BREEDER OF MAINE COON CATS

ROBIN SCHWARTZ
Potatoes and Stigby
Hoboken, New Jersey, 1995

That Barn Cat

John Drysdale
Kitten Makes an Ass of Itself
Glamorgan, Wales, 1981

There's a cat in love with my horse Harpo these days. The cat is a big old barn tom, but Harpo's a Thoroughbred, and was pretty high-strung until the cat came around. In the morning when I go to feed him that cat is always lying in the feed bin. If Harpo lies down for a nap, the cat lies down between his front legs, and Harpo is very careful not to move them. They play hide-and-seek out in the field: Harpo nickers and lowers his nose to the grass and the cat meows and pounces. Thing is, this cat doesn't give a hoot about any other animals—not the dog or the other cats, or even the other horses. Harpo is it. And if I go for a ride, I can lift the cat up with me and he'll stay on the whole way. I hold the cat and the cat holds Harpo, holding onto the mane with his teeth.

ANNE FORELLI, RESEARCH BIOLOGIST

Sympathy Cat

Walter Chandoha
Chiara and Ginger
Annandale, New Jersey, 1966

The year after my mother died, I would stay home alone on the weekends just trying to deal with it. I had this one cat named Nori-San who was black with a white triangle on his chest. He had green eyes and a sweet little voice. Normally he was pretty friendly—nothing remarkable. But during this time he became extremely loving. He'd come and nuzzle me or lick my ear, or he'd try to distract me with his antics. He'd keep at it until I cheered up. Once I got over my blue period, he reverted back to his old self, stealing my jewelry and hiding it under the sofa. One morning at 4 a.m. I realized I'd lost my watch and when Nori-San ran by, he had the watch in his mouth. I followed him into the living room and under the couch he had this little stash. There was everything I thought I'd lost. And he was perfectly willing to give it back. He was a very special cat.

Missy Rogers, clothing designer

PER WICHMANN
In the Field (series)
Sweden, 1989

KRITINA LEE KNIEF
Sinbad and Alfie
Hoboken, New Jersey, 1989

Opposite:
ROBIN SCHWARTZ
Noah and Nathaniel
Hoboken, New Jersey, 1995

Josephine

THOMAS WESTER
Norwegian Fisherman and His Ca[...]
Vaeroy Lofoten, Norway, 1974

My cat saved my life. Not directly, but just by being her. When I was in the hospital, I was in a very sedated state for a while. I must have been told that I might not come out of it, because I was vaguely conscious that death was a prospect. I remember having end-of-life kind of dreams.

In my hazy state I sort of reviewed in my mind all the people I knew—my friends and relations. And I came to the conclusion that everybody would survive this. And then I got to my own family. I got to my kitten, Terry, and concluded that she was young enough to survive this. But then I got to Josephine, the older cat. What about Josephine? That question was ringing in my ears. I don't know what the timing of this was, but the doctor later told me that just about when he'd given up all hope, I turned around and started fighting for my life. And I figured out later that it was on the same day as I thought about Josephine that there was a change in all those dial readings.

I can't know for certain that the thought and the improvement were connected. But it seems to me that this was the only notion I had that said, "Charles, you have to pull out of this." As I say this, Josephine's sitting on my lap. She's sprawled out with one nail dug right into my skin through the ankle, and the other dug into the leather of my shoe. This is how she spends a lot of her time. Ever since I came back from the hospital, she's been more affectionate than she'd ever been before. She started this habit of following me everywhere. She will not let me out of her sight. If I have to go somewhere, she's invariably inside the door to the garage when I come back, and she gives me kind of a "whough"— almost like a bark. She absolutely thinks that I'm her person. I don't think anyone who's been near us has any doubt about that.

CHARLES SHEROVER, PHILOSOPHER

ROBIN SCHWARTZ
Teddy and Katja
Massachusetts, 1988

JOHN DRYSDALE
Tom and Jerry Sharing
Kings Lynn, Norfolk,
England, 1970

Sinbad

HAROLD M. LAMBERT
The Grooming Session
Philadelphia, c.1950

My cat Sinbad, who I got when he was a kitten along with his sister Salem, does this loving gesture I've never seen before: he sucks on my ear. I can hold him in my arms like a baby and he'll lean into my neck and suckle on my ear. It's a very intimate gesture. He can stay there for hours, completely content. Then he goes and finds Salem and they curl up together like a yin-yang symbol.

JENNIFER CHARLES, RECORDING ARTIST

THOMAS WESTER
Maj Stina Larsson
Yttemas Roslagen,
Sweden, 1984

Said the Parrot to the Pussycat

Robin Schwartz
Ricky and Tequilla
Teaneck, New Jersey, 1995

I adopted a gray tabby, one of those remote, attractive types that won't tell you how they're feeling. I named him Redford. And I brought him into a house that already had a dog, Oprah, and a parrot named Cassandra. I was a little nervous about creating my own food chain, so I tried to keep them separated. Redford and Oprah kept their distance, but Redford would not stay away from Cassandra. Her cage was in the living room and that's where he wanted to be. He was fascinated by her. I was really nervous I'd come home from work to a mess of feathers.

One day I was in the living room when Redford came in. Cassandra had her eye on him too. She cocked her head in that "I see you" way. I held my breath. And what did Redford do? He jumped onto the edge of the sofa and hooked a claw into Cassandra's cage to hold it fast. If the cage door opened, death in a minute. But Cassandra? She made this noise. Not an alarm but a low chirp. Kind of seductive. She sidestepped down her perch toward the cat. Stupid bird! Then they touched noses. Or beak and nose. I couldn't believe this! They did it again and again.

"Cassandra," I called out. "Are you all right?" Usually I'd get an answer. But Cassandra was busy. Redford was purring and turning his head upside down to get a different look at her and she was delighted. She poked lightly at him with her beak and fluttered her wings prettily and bobbed up and down. Then I understood. Maybe poor Redford had a parrot in his previous life. Maybe Cassandra didn't know any better. But there was no food chain involved.

Their attachment deepened. She'd leave her cage to be at his side. They ate together, talked together, slept—spent almost all their time together. Cassandra would settle next to Redford and he'd put his arm around her. They were so gentle you'd swear they were under a spell. I wish I had a picture.

Tessa Smith, ACTRESS

Tender Ziggy

THOMAS WESTER
Curious Man and Cat
Stockholm, Sweden, 1988

My sister has this old cat named Ziggy, a big fat alley cat. He's usually very disdainful and haughty when there are a lot of people in a room. He either glares at you or makes himself scarce. Well, one day I was visiting and was only one of many people in the room, so of course the cat was being very snooty and I was being snooty back. Then, suddenly, everyone else walked out. We were alone. I was on the sofa, he was prowling the floor. And I have to say that he made the first move. He climbed up to me and put his paws on my shoulders, just like an embrace, and then he just stared me in the face. I felt an intense love coming from him then. We touched noses in a delicate, intimate gesture. Then someone came into the room and it was over. I guess he only loves people one on one, in private. Then he's actually very tender.

SPENCER BECK, WRITER

The Profound Feline

John Drysdale
*Kitten with
Powerful Friendship
Welwyn Garden City,
England, 1979*

To think that cats don't have wonderful feelings is human arrogance. We're mammals, cats are mammals; we all have these feelings because we are mammals, not because we are people. And think of it: love has powerful evolutionary value—for those whose system requires them to keep together and cooperate, positive feelings for each other will make life go so much more smoothly. In our culture, we put tremendous importance on romantic love. But friendship-based love can be very strong—the love between siblings, parent and child, companions. Even in long-standing couples, that's the glue that holds us together—and cats too. One kind of love is more stormy, the other is more profound. Perhaps we could say that cats are more profound.

Elizabeth Marshall Thomas,
anthropologist and author

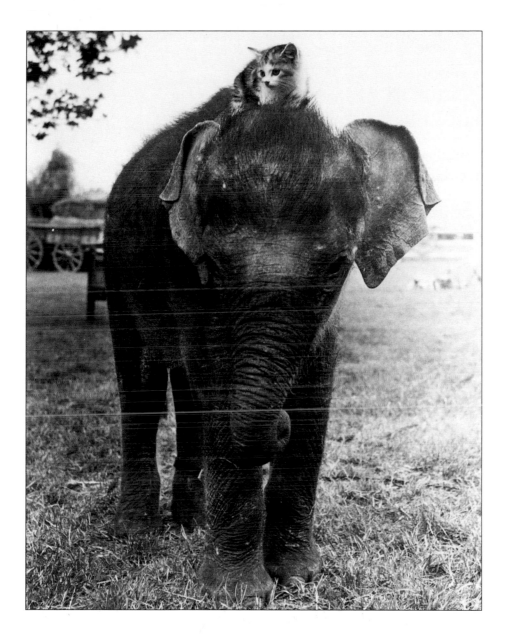

ROBIN SCHWARTZ
Jonah and Noah
Hoboken, New Jersey, 1993

The Easter Cat

I always had rabbits. Then my friend's cat had kittens and I took a little white one because it looked the most like a rabbit. The kitten, Lily, grew up with rabbits hopping around. I think she knew she was not a rabbit, but she may still not know that they are not cats. As a youth Lily pulled some great capers with the bunnies—playing chase games all over the house, wrestling, nestling up to sleep with them. But she grew up to be as big as the rabbits. She could easily hurt one. Instead she guards them with great concern. If one strays into the yard, she keeps watch to make sure none of the other cats around the neighborhood mess with it. If one of the rabbits gets startled, she lies down next to it and her warmth seems to calm it down.

One time a rabbit got stuck behind the refrigerator and couldn't get out, and Lily came to my study and harassed me until I had to stop working. She leaped onto the desk and skidded into all my papers— which she knows is a bad move— and made a big racket. I finally got up and went into the kitchen to see if she was out of food. But she wasn't. Instead she led me to the refrigerator and then tried to get behind it. I thought maybe she'd lost a toy, but instead I found one of my rabbits. Or should I say our rabbits. If I hadn't have found the rabbit, it could have died.

KELLY CORE, FINANCIAL PLANNER

JOHN DRYSDALE
Peaceful Coexistence
Kings Lynn, Norfolk,
England, 1970

Overleaf:
THOMAS WESTER
Elsie Wigh
Grabo, Sweden, 1984

Don Gato of W. 105th Street

MARY BLOOM
Meri and Kitten
Sharon, Connecticut, 1983

When I lived in Spanish Harlem, I had a cat who was clearly in love with my girlfriend. Even after we got him fixed, he'd get all aroused. Every night he would come into bed and move against her. He was definitely a passionate cat. One day he was resting on the windowsill and it started to rain. I was asleep under the window. In a half-conscious state I reached up to close it and instead of coming in the cat jumped out—three flights down. He wound up hanging around in the backyard having a quick fling with a girl cat, and then came back up three days later, completely unhurt. He was hungry, but he was happy. And he stopped bothering my girlfriend.

BEN PEROWSKI, DRUMMER

Love to a Cat

KRITINA LEE KNIEF
Muppet-Faced
Mother and Kitten
Boston, 1991

This is how I see it: cats pretend they don't need anybody's love. This makes us feel incredibly insecure and then we lavish all this extra attention on them and then they get annoyed and reject us. Spurned like this we try even harder—special treats, extrasoft blankets, total clemency when they bring in dead birds. We decide another cat in the house might make them feel less lonely. So one day we bring in their new companion and all hell breaks loose. Our cat becomes a bully and chases the newcomer under the sofa. Our cat makes us feel awful for disrespecting her sovereignty over our house. So we feel guilty. We obsess over our latest infractions. We talk about nothing else. At the water cooler in the office, at the gym, on the phone: we confess our guilt and wonder how we will get rid of the intruder. We spend lunches finding a new home for this second-class cat. We find one and feel great—life will calm down again and our cat will be grateful for our getting rid of this problem and will become more affectionate, surely.

Then we get home to make everything nice and ready for the new owner to come for their new cat. But there is silence in the house. Both cats are hiding. See, in our absence, they have bonded. They are now inseparable. They refuse to be divided, spend every minute with each other, sleep in mirror images of each other, purr only for each other, and are united forever in their solemn pact to completely ignore us except for a perfunctory moment at mealtime. That is love, so far as I can tell, to a cat. No matter what we do, we are still left out of the picture. But actually, that's only my version. I hear of loving feline-human relationships all the time. It's just that my cats haven't.

RICHARD S., POET

The Cat Who Came to Work

THOMAS WESTER
Untitled
Stockholm, Sweden, 1984

Of all the cats I've ever known, Polar Star is the most lovable. He's named after Polar Bear, the cat who came for Christmas, who was also a wonderful cat but in a different way. Polar Star is also white, a big guy with six toes on each paw. Someone on Martha's Vineyard just threw him out of her house at the end of the summer. And now I want her to know what she's missing, because he's the most all-around lovable cat I have seen in my life. When I first met him, he came and put his paw on me, and I was blown away. I always tease people that they taught him to do that. The Board members love him. The whole office loves him. Anyone who comes in, Polar Star has to sit in their lap and find out what they're up to. Since he's been here, more than 300 people have asked me if they could adopt him. But I'd never give him up. He's affectionate, philosophical and sweet: everything you could ever want in one cat.

CLEVELAND AMORY, PRESIDENT AND FOUNDER, THE FUND FOR ANIMALS

Maurice

Maurice's mother climbed into my lap to have him and three other kittens. Maurice slept with me every night from that day until he was well into his second year. One day, I had to go to Puerto Rico for a long weekend to work on a film. When I got back, he seemed totally disheveled and bleary-eyed. Unused to sleeping by himself, he had paced around the whole time.

As he got older he grew quite large, to about twenty pounds. And he was clumsy. Whenever he'd see me, he'd flip over on his back and the whole room would shake.

Needless to say, he slept with me for the rest of his life.

J.C. SUARÈS

Grinch and the Burmese

WALTER CHANDOHA
City Courtship on 46th Street
New York, 1950

The animal clinic I work in got in a burly cat that was part Persian and all grump. A tooth infection made him so irritable he hated to be touched—though his owner said that was nothing new. His nickname was Grinch. After surgery I put him in the cat room in a quiet cage next to a little Burmese that ignored everyone. She was a sad little cat: her owner was away on business a lot, and the cat boarded here. It didn't seem like much of a life.

When I went to check on Grinch's recovery I thought, "Well, he'll probably be in a really bad mood." I shoved my hands into my pockets to keep myself from reflexively reaching for him and getting clawed, and walked into the cat room. There was Grinch, sitting up with his eyes shut, purring so loudly the cage rattled. His lips were curled into a funny smile and his tongue was hanging out. His paws did little kneading motions into the blanket.

I was really worried. Did I have a stoned cat on my hands? Had I given him too much anesthetic? I checked the dosage, but it was right. Then I noticed the little Burmese—she was kind of hidden, crouching right next to him. She was grooming him through the bars. This was the source of Grinch's bliss. He lay down like a majestic lion and the Burmese followed, pressing herself closely against him. They turned their heads towards each other as if they were lovers inhaling each other's wonderful scents. They slept all day like that.

The next morning, when Grinch's owner came to get him, he hissed at her. He yowled from his crate and the Burmese yowled back. It was cacaphony. None of us knew what to do. Home, he hid from his owner and scratched up the furniture. And the Burmese, here, went on a hunger strike.

But this story has a happy ending. Grinch's owner, desperate to have a mellower cat, offered to take the Burmese. The Burmese's owner agreed to let her cat go live with Grinch. Now Grinch has no more tantrums, and the Burmese is sleek and fat. If one has to go to the vet, they come together. The Burmese needed to stay overnight recently and Grinch stayed with her. They were in heaven. It was like a second honeymoon.

CHRISTOPHER KALLINI,
VETERINARY ASSISTANT

Staying Objective

PATRICIA MCENERY
David and Assistant
Beaulieu, France 1996

I certainly believe that my cats love me. It would be very strange every time my cat jumps on my lap to just have some objective thought about the cat just wanting to keep warm or whatever. I had three cats—I lost one in December. And my little one, who's between five and six years old now, has actually become much more affectionate and entertaining in the past couple of months—much more attached to me, I think. My male cat, Ollie, whom I've had since he was six weeks, sleeps in my arms every night. When I'm home he's invariably on my lap and has an incredibly loud purr. I have a recliner—it's his chair, but he lets me sit in it. Whenever I do, which is a lot, he'll stand up, put his paws around my neck, and purr into my ear. It that a nonemotional response?

R. LEE ZASLOFF, PH.D., ASSOCIATE DIRECTOR, CENTER FOR ANIMALS AND SOCIETY, UNIVERSITY OF CALIFORNIA AT DAVIS

Silence of a Siamese

KRITINA LEE KNIEF
Jasmine and Sabu
Chicago, 1991

My neighbor has a Siamese, Ethel Merman, who is very vocal. I can hear them talking to each other. He's been sick, and recently had to leave for a week to have some tests, and I fed Ethel Merman. Everyday I'd let myself in and walk into my neighbor's kitchen and Ethel would come running in, chattering away. Then she'd stop and give me this look. Just a long, steady look. And she'd be silent until I left. When he came back, the reunion was very emotional. I know. I heard it.

RITSUKO UCHIDA, ARTIST

The Cat and the Grizzly

We're a twenty-four-acre wildlife care center that takes in wild animals exclusively. But people with kittens who haven't got the heart to take them to a pound where they might be euthanized often bring them here. "Bring" is a relative term, but we always try to live-trap them and, through a network of some 100 volunteers, get even the wildest ones spayed, neutered, and placed. Some months ago, someone threw a boxful over our fence. We managed to trap three of them, but somehow one little rascal got away.

Where he wound up was sheer luck on his part. He got into the grizzly bear's compound—the one bear out of sixteen bears here that would probably tolerate him. This bear came to us as an orphaned cub in 1990, after being struck by a train in Montana. He'd been res-cued by a Blackfeet Indian, lain unconscious for six days, spent time in a Montana hospital's intensive care unit, and wound up blind in his right eye with neuro-logical damage. He was too habitu-ated to humans and too mentally impaired to go back to the wild, so we got him.

Grizzly bears are not generally social creatures. Except for when they mate or raise cubs, they're loners. I'd generally spend some time with Griz to give him some interpersonal attention, and late one July afternoon I approached his cage as usual. He'd just been served his normal mix—vegeta-bles, fruit, dog kibble, fish, and chicken—and was lying down with the bucket between his forepaws and eating when I saw a little spot of orange coming out of the black-berry brambles. It was a tiny kit-ten—no more than six weeks old and about twelve ounces at the most—the missing one from the brood we'd found the week before. I wasn't sure if I should run in and try to rescue him because I was afraid he'd panic and run straight for Griz. So I just stood back and watched things develop.

The kitten (who we named Cat) approached the bear and let out a purr and a mew, and the bear looked at him, grabbed a piece of chicken out of the bucket, and threw it towards him with his forepaw. Cat carried it into the bushes to eat. I suspect he'd been there about a week since he was in better shape than his siblings had been when we found them.

Two weeks later, I saw Cat feeding with Griz again. This time he was rubbing and purring against him, and Griz reached down and picked him up by the scruff of his neck. After that, the friendship seemed to blossom. Especially during the kit-

ten stages, it was really cute to see. Cat would eat with Griz, rub up against him, bat him on the nose, ambush him, sleep with him. And though Griz is a gentle bear, a bear's gentleness is not that gentle. Once he once stepped on Cat accidentally and looked horrified to realize he'd done it. And sometimes still when he tries to pick up Cat by the scruff, he winds up picking up Cat's whole head. But Cat doesn't seem to mind. He just licks himself clean again, because I don't think he likes to have his fur wet. And though he's been doing a little tomcatting in the middle of the night lately—which we decided not to stop since it might change everything—he still seeks out Griz's company. It's great to see how well these two guys get along.

DAVE SIDDON, FOUNDER, WILDLIFE
IMAGES REHABILITATION CENTER

How to Bond with a Dog

THOMAS WESTER
Natural Enemies
Stockholm, Sweden, 1984

One of my own cats, a champagne tabby named Stain, fell in love with my dog over the course of a month when they were both in the house a lot. It was the rainy season in Arizona, and the animals preferred the confines of the house to the stormy outside. Stain had never given the dog much attention. But suddenly, he seemed overcome by an incredible desire to spend every minute, waking or not, at her side. She is a gentle, playful German Shepherd, more curious than aggressive. At first she'd lie on the floor, her side against the front door in her customary way, and Stain would come marching up, his tail held kitten-high, and head right for her face. He'd brush himself against her two or three times until finally she gave him a lick. Thus encouraged, he'd come back for more, beginning to purr and playfully box her nose with a paw, until finally she began to wag her tail. When he sensed she'd accepted him, he steadied himself and jumped clear onto her back, wedging himself between dog and door. If she got up to find privacy, he'd rush between her legs, slowing her down, lying on his back and poking up at her. After a week, she relented. From then on she expected him to be at her side, and he was. At mealtimes, on walks, even when I took her for a jog—Stain would follow close behind, never letting her out of his adoring sight.

JANE MARTIN

Overleaf:
THOMAS WESTER
Natural Enemies Continued
Stockholm, Sweden, 1984

Mochi the Jungle Cat

PER WICHMANN
Kittens
Stockholm, Sweden, 1990

We come here maybe twice a year, more if we can get the time from touring, and our shack in the jungle is empty except for then. Mochi is a jungle cat, the same mixture of tortoiseshell and Siamese that a lot of cats in Puna, Hawaii, are—small and fierce, strong enough to kill a mongoose or a rat and live for days on nothing.

When we get here, she suddenly shows up. Every year. No one else ever sees her. And every year she shows up pregnant, as if she times her litters for our arrival, knowing somehow that when we're around, there's good food and good care. She moves right in in her quiet, sweet way, never pushing us, never demanding, just watching. Her belly swells bigger and bigger and of course we hand her all the extras from whatever meal we've made, and she never gets fussy or upset.

We are her guardians—her midwives—she seems to be saying, and she pays us back in affection. One by one on the first days we're all together here, she climbs into our laps and welcomes us. Then the routine is exactly as it has always been. The day we are all scheduled to leave, she has her kittens. There's a box downstairs, an old banana box, and it's been the same box every year since this started. I have no idea how she knows it's our time to go, but that's when she drops. She shows us her kittens and has one last big meal. Then she takes them and heads back into the jungle, and we head back to touring, knowing we'll see her again.

JOHN MEDESKI, MUSICIAN

WALTER CHANDOHA
Farm Kittens
Landisville, New Jersey, 1954

Opposite:
WALTER CHANDOHA
Kissing Cousins
Huntington, Long Island, 1959

Romance

ROBIN SCHWARTZ
Noah and Nathaniel
Hoboken, New Jersey, 1994

I know cats feel differently. But they have their own kind of romance. When they fall in love, it's deeply. The Big Daddy around my house is Sir Oliver, a handsome and distinguished tabby who loves attention. One of my females, Glistening Sylvia, is an absolute flirt at nine years old, and she will not leave Oliver alone. She hugs him, kisses him, tries to snuggle underneath him when he naps, and follows him everywhere. When he requests a little privacy by putting out a paw, she sits a few feet away and stares at him adoringly. When they lie together on the throw rug in the hall, she'll growl to keep everyone else away. She wants him for himself, and I think he loves it. I've never seen him admonish her.

MARGE BEEBE, ANIMAL BEHAVIORIST
AND BREEDER OF MAINE COON CATS

Buddies

John Drysdale
Wild Relationship
Market Drayton,
England, 1972

Varner and Akbar are kind of cool cucumbers. I mean if there's an animal they want to hunt down and kill, they get crazed over that. I've certainly known cats that were total mushpots, but not my guys. Of course I know they love each other. They are out-and-out buddies. And I know they love us. But I couldn't quite prove it.

Constance Herndon, editor

The Girl Next Door

DONNA RUSKIN
Untitled
New York, 1989

One of my cats had an affair with the female kitten next door. It was a presexual, childhood affair. They would romp and cuddle. But as soon as she got fixed, he stopped getting along with her. She seemed devastated for about a day. She came to my door and wailed. Then the next day she had a new beau.

ANNE MARLOWE, WRITER

Acknowledgments

The editor would like to thank all those
who contributed their stories to this book,
with special gratitude to
Cleveland Amory of the Fund for Animals,
Elizabeth Marshall Thomas,
R. Lee Zasloff of the Center for Animals and
Society, University of California at Davis,
and Charles Sherover.

Photo Credits

Indicia

Designed and edited by J.C. Suarès
Text compiled and edited by Jane Martin
Design Assistance by Christy Trotter
Drawings by J.C. Suarès